The Seven Last Words of Our Lord
Upon the Cross

The Seven Last Words of Our Lord Upon the Cross

By the Servant of God Mother Catherine Abrikosova, T.O.S.D.

Translated by Joseph Lake
and Brendan D. King

Edited by Brendan D. King

ST. AUGUSTINE'S PRESS
South Bend, Indiana

Manufactured in the United States of America.

1 2 3 4 5 6   25 24 23 22 21 20 19

**Library of Congress Control Number:
2019934705**

∞ The paper used in this publication meets the
minimum requirements of the American National
Standard for Information Sciences - Permanence
of Paper for Printed Materials, ANSI Z39.48-
1984.

St. Augustine's Press
www.staugustine.net

Preface
By Brendan D. King

Mother Catherine Abrikosova's *"The Seven Last Words of Our Lord Upon the Cross"* has been called the most remarkable work of Catholic literature ever written in the Russian language. It is not difficult to understand why.

Offering a balance between Dominican and Eastern Christian theology, Mother Catherine leads the reader down a carefully defined path of spiritual Crucifixion, mystical death, and Resurrection unto the life of the Divine. Along the way, she covers seven topics: love for one's enemies, repentance, detachment, despondence, spiritual thirst, gratitude to the Redeemer, and the Great Calm of unity with Christ. Each of these chapters remains as relevant to twenty-first-century Catholics as when they were first penned, in the aftermath of the

Russian Revolution, by a Byzantine Catholic nun and former Marxist.

Anna Ivanovna Abrikosova was born into a wealthy and cultured family of Moscow industrialists and philanthropists on January 23, 1882.[1] After spending her entire adult life as an agnostic, she was received into the Catholic Church in Paris on December 20, 1908.

On August 4, 1917,[2] a mere three months before the Bolsheviks seized power in Petrograd, Anna founded a Byzantine Catholic convent of the Third Order Regular of Saint Dominic inside her Moscow apartment. Taking the name Mother Catherine of Siena, she and her whole community offered themselves as a sacrifice, unto the last drop of blood, for the salvation of Russia and for priests. It was to the sisters of her convent that Mother Catherine's meditation on "The Seven Last Words" was first addressed.

---

1   According to the Julian Calendar, which is still used by the Russian Orthodox Church.
2   Also according to the Julian Calendar, which was then used by Russia's Byzantine Catholics with Papal assent. At the time, August 4 was the Feast of Saint Dominic.

Anyone who reads Mother Catherine's meditation should always remember the backdrop against which it was written.

Beginning in 1922, anti-religious carnivals filled the streets of Moscow every Easter and Christmas. Parade floats and street theatre hurled gratuitous insults at every past and present religious belief. Teenaged members of the Young Communist League, or Komsomol, vandalized churches and disrupted services with chants of, "Down with the priests! Down with the monks! We shall climb the heavens and chase away the gods!" As a climax, Christ, His Blessed Mother, Allah, and Yahweh were burned in effigy as Komsomol members danced around the flames, swilled vodka, and sang blasphemous parodies of Christmas carols.[3]

All this has an oddly contemporary feel, but Lenin's Bolsheviks did not confine themselves to vandalism and mockery. Under the pretext of "famine relief", church buildings

3   Paul Gabel, *And God Created Lenin: Marxism vs. Religion in Russia, 1917–1929* (Amherst, New York: Prometheus Books, 2005), pp. 170–72.

were looted by the police and confiscated by the State. Those which were not torn down were transformed into concert halls, dance halls, and anti-religious museums.[4] Clergy, monks, nuns, and thousands of ordinary believers were being arrested, executed after cursory trials, or sent to die a slow death in Arctic concentration camps.[5]

Teaching religion to minors had just been made a criminal offense.[6] Therefore, Mother Catherine's decision to secretly open a Catholic school would eventually have made her convent a target. But the Soviet State feared nothing so much as the world outside its borders. Therefore, it was Mother Catherine's loyalty to both the Roman Pontiff and the traditions of the Russian Church that truly put her into the crosshairs of the Soviet secret police.

---

4   Father Christopher Lawrence Zugger, *The Forgotten: Catholics in the Soviet Empire from Lenin through Stalin* (Syracuse, NY: University of Syracuse Press, 2001), p. 172.

5   Alexander Solzhenitsyn, *The GULAG Archipelago: An Experiment in Literary Investigation* (New York: Harper & Rowe Publishers, 1973), pp. 36–38.

6   Ibid., pp. 37–38.

She cannot have known that the chapel's confessional had been bugged. She did not know that novice monk Pavel Shafirov, whose show of piety so edified everyone, was an informer. She did know, however, that the arrest of her whole community was a foregone conclusion. Therefore, Mother Catherine wrote her sole surviving spiritual work to prepare the sisters of her convent for what was coming.

At 11:00 p.m. on Wednesday, November 8, 1923, the sisters heard a long expected-knock on their door. When it was opened, the convent was invaded by a posse of secret police agents and Red Army soldiers with drawn revolvers.

According to Father Edmund J. Walsh, the American Jesuit charged with overseeing the Vatican's Famine Relief Mission, "They gathered all the sisters in one room and kept them there until 5:30 the next morning, subjecting all to a most savage interrogation, casting ridicule and scorn on their religious practices and generally terrorizing the community … After a night of agony, they brought an automobile and carried off Madame A[brikosov] and seven or eight sisters. At the same time, similar searches and arrests were made in the homes of parishioners."[7]

In July 1924, the sisters were assembled in Moscow's Butyrka Prison and informed that they had been tried and convicted by a special tribunal of the Soviet secret police. The charges not only included "organizing illegal schools for the education of children in a religious-fascist spirit", but also conspiring to violently overthrow the Soviet Government. Their co-conspirators were alleged to be the Vatican, the Romanov pretender, the Governments of Poland and Lithuania, "The Supreme Monarchist Council", and "international fascism." Mother Catherine was sentenced to ten years of solitary confinement. The remaining sisters were sentenced to terms of imprisonment or exile in villages above the Arctic Circle.

Sister Philomena Ejsmont, who was present at the sentencing, later wrote that Mother Catherine and her spiritual daughters received

7 *The Russian Revolution and Religion: A Collection of Documents Concerning the Suppression of Religion by the Communists. 1917-1925,* translated and edited by Boleslaw Szczesniak (Notre Dame, IN: University of Notre Dame Press, 1959), p. 219.

their unjust sentences with joy. Certain that their offer to sacrifice themselves for Russia had been accepted, they chanted the *"Te Deum"* in Old Slavonic,[8] the liturgical language of the Russian Church. Soon after, the sisters were taken to their separate places of imprisonment and Siberian exile.

During her solitary confinement at Yaroslavl, Mother Catherine used her supervised walks around the prison yard as an opportunity to counsel and evangelize her fellow prisoners. According to her spiritual director, she also offered her loneliness and sufferings from cancer as an unceasing prayer for her brother, Dr. Alexei Ivanovich Abrikosov. A pillar of the Soviet medical profession, Alexei had left his wife for another woman, married her in a civil ceremony, and published a repudiation of Christianity in the Soviet press.

In August 1932, Mother Catherine underwent an operation for breast cancer in Butyrka Prison. Having learned of this, the wife of

---

8   In the Russian Church, the *Te Deum* is known under its Old Slavonic title, *Тебе Бога Хвалим*, (*Tebe Boga Hvalim*).

acclaimed author Maxim Gorky intervened with Soviet Premier Joseph Stalin, who granted Mother Catherine early release. Also at the instigation of Gorky's wife, the Soviet State offered the released prisoner an exit visa, assuming that she would leave for the West and cause them no further trouble.

To Mother Catherine, however, accepting this offer would have meant violating the promise she had made to God. She indignantly refused to leave Russia, re-established contact with the surviving sisters, and joined a secret effort to spread the Catholic faith among Komsomol members and university students. When her cancer resumed, a fellow sister warned her of the risks she was taking. Mother Catherine responded, "For the good and for the salvation of a single soul I am willing to go to prison for another ten years."

On August 5, 1933, the Soviet secret police arrested Mother Catherine at Kostroma, where she had chosen to live after her release. She was transported to Moscow under guard and again confined at Butyrka Prison. There, she was joined by the sisters of her community and many other Byzantine Catholic priests, laity, and religious.

On January 10, 1934, sentences were again handed down. The accused were all declared guilty of forming a terrorist organization, planning to assassinate Stalin, and impose a British-style constitutional monarchy and "Papal Theocracy" on Soviet Russia. Even though her cancer was known to be terminal, Mother Catherine was sentenced to eight years of solitary confinement and returned to Yaroslavl. The sisters of her community were never to see her again.

Mother Catherine Abrikosova died of cancer in the infirmary of Butyrka Prison on June 23, 1936. After an autopsy established the cause of death as a malignant tumor based in the sacral bone at the base of the spine, her body was loaded into an apple crate and taken by truck to Moscow's Donskoy Cemetery. There, she was taken to the cellars of the former Orthodox Church of Saint Seraphim of Sarov, which had been converted into a crematorium by the Soviet government. After her body was reduced to ash, agents of the secret police cast her earthly remains into a mass grave with tens of thousands of other sets of ashes.

In 1942, the pit was paved over with

asphalt and another mass grave was dug.[9] Shortly before the collapse of the U.S.S.R. in 1991, a gravestone was erected, inscribed with the words: "Here lie the innocent, tortured, and executed victims of the political repressions of 1930–1942. Let their Memory be Eternal!"[10]

The last word is best left to Mother Catherine herself: "The soul is at the dawn, at the threshold of unity and the fullness of life. And she awaits her time in peace and calm ...

"He shall come with the dawn of the Third Day, shining in glory, to lead the soul, joyful and free, into His Bridal Chamber. Yet He has left her to rest for a time. She has suffered together with her Crucified God. She has struggled and, in spite of all things; the pressures of the world, the flesh and the Devil, she has remained faithful. She has hoped. She has loved.

---

9   David Remnick, *Lenin's Tomb: The Last Days of the Soviet Empire* (New York: Vintage Books, 1994), pp. 136–38.

10 Stephen F. Cohen, *The Victims Return: Survivors of the Gulag after Stalin* (Exeter, NH: Publishing Works, 2010), p. 144. The inscription has been re-translated based on photographs.

"And now is her victory, having conquered the world. Now, together with her Lord, she has merited her rest.

"The night is come. Around the Cross *'a Great Calm'* has descended. It is the Sabbath Day, when the Lord rested from all His Works. Jesus gazes peacefully and clearly at the heavens and quietly says, as He had when a child: *'Father, into Thy Hands I commend My Spirit.' And having said this, He bowed His Head and gave up the Ghost.'"*

—Saint Cloud, Minnesota
March 24, 2016

Primary Sources.

* Mother Catherine Abrikosova (1922), Letter to Fr. Bede Jarrett, O.P., the Dominican Provincial of England, about the Foundation of the Community. The original text in English has not been located, but a translation into French was published in the 1922 edition of *"L'Annee Dominicaine,"* Paris 34, Rue du Bac. Pages 203-04.

* Sister Philomena Ejsmont (1987), *"The Moscow Third Order Sisters of the Eastern-Slavonic Rite,"* Prof. Joseph Lake's unpublished English translation, based on photocopies of the original handwritten memoir in the private archive of Father Georgii Friedman in Moscow.

* Fr. Ambrosius K. Eszer, O.P. (1970), *"Eka-terina Sienskaja (Anna I.) Abrikosova und die Gemeinschaft der Schwestern des III. Ordens von Heiligen Dominikus zu Moskau,"*

"Archivum Fratrum Praedicatorum," Volume XL. Pages 277–373.

* Anatolia Nowicka (1989), *"Memoir from the History of the Moscow Chapter of the Sisters of St. Dominic, 1921-1932,"* Translated from the original Polish by Claire S. Allen and published by *"The Sarmatian Review,"* September, 1989. Pages 1–15.

* Irina Osipova (2001), *"Hide Me Within Thy Wounds: The Persecution of the Catholic Church in the USSR,"* Germans from Russia Heritage Collection, Fargo, North Dakota.

* Irina Osipova (2014), *"Brides of Christ, Martyrs for Russia: Mother Catherine Abrikosova and the Eastern Rite Dominican Sisters,"* Translated and self-published by Dr. Geraldine Kelley of Colorado.

* Pavel Parfentiev (2004), *"Мать Екатерина (А. И. Абрикосова) Жизнь и Служение,"* St. Petersburg. An authorized, but unpublished, English translation has been produced by Prof. Joseph Lake, Ph.D.

* Fr. Christopher Lawrence Zugger (2001), *"The Forgotten: Catholics in the Soviet Empire from Lenin through Stalin,"* University of Syracuse Press.

"The Seven Last Words of Our Lord upon the Cross"[*]
By Mother Catherine Abrikosova

Introduction

Every soul truly wishing to attain the blessed state in which she may say together with the Holy Apostle Paul, *"I live, now not I, but Christ liveth in me"* (Gal. 2:20), must live her life through the Passion of Our Lord Jesus Christ.

[*] First Published as *"Последние слова Господа нашего на Кресте"* in the journal *"Символ,"* No. 41, July 1999, Paris, pp. 249–85. Based on a hand-written copy, which miraculously escaped being destroyed by Stalin's secret police, and which is currently preserved in the private archive of Fr. Georgii Friedman in Moscow.—The Editor.

Fix your gaze upon your wounded Lord Jesus, and upon Him alone. Strive tirelessly with all your might to attain Him, God made man, in such a way that you acquire knowledge of His Divinity through His wounded humanity. Christ, and Him Crucified, is all our knowledge and all our life. This is truth because Christ came to earth in order to transfigure unto the supernatural state, to grant us the ability to participate in His own Beatific Life and to impart towards us the greatest happiness and joy possible. These we achieve by glorifying His Holy Name, living and suffering selflessly, and keeping our eyes fixed upon His glory alone. But all the earthly life of the Lord leads to the Cross and is concentrated upon it. The glory of the Resurrection comes by way of Golgotha, and it is this which characterizes the life our souls.

The Lord is not merely our Savior and Redeemer. He is also Priest, meaning above all Teacher, for He is both the Wisdom and Word of the Father.

"Heaven and earth shall pass away, but my words shall not pass away" (Mark 13:31). Every word of Jesus is like to a creative act. He generates, creates, and carries within Himself

the seal of eternity and there is no doubt that His highest teaching chair was the Cross. It is as though He gathered His entire self upon the Cross and delivered all Himself over to us: *"And I, if I be lifted up from the earth, will draw all men to Myself"* (John 12:32). He taught above all through His silence. Quiet contemplation of our silent and crucified God is the best means to permeate ourselves with the soul of Christ.

Furthermore, it was from His Cross that He gave His last will and testament to us. This testament is contained in His Seven Last Words. Within them, He included all that our souls need to fully bloom, attain sanctity, and to glorify His Father in Heaven. The glorification of the Father is what delights the Most Holy Heart[1] of Jesus.

"Father! Glorify Thy Name." (John 12:28). This was His favorite prayer. He came

---

1   As Mother Catherine Abrikosova was a Byzantine Catholic, I have chosen to use Eastern Christian terminology whenever possible. Hence "Most Holy Heart" instead of Sacred Heart, "Most Pure Heart" instead of Immaculate Heart, and "Mysteries" instead of Sacraments.—The Editor.

unto the earth that, having elevated mankind unto the supernatural life, He could bring them to a new knowledge. The life of man is for the glory of God and that the chief motivation of man should be this prayer of Jesus: *"Father! Glorify Thy Name."*

When we behold Golgotha we see creation: hostile or friendly, we also see our fellow creature in all His attributes. We also behold God—the Omnipotent wellspring and destination of all mankind. Lastly, we behold Jesus Christ the Priest and Intermediary uplifted between the heavens and the earth, between the Father and His works, and stretched upon His highest teaching chair, upon His Cross. From His Cross He spoke Seven Words and, with these Words, He places us in our true and proper relationship to God, to creation, and, in consequence, to ourselves. Within them lies His entire testament, for He knew that without this threefold relationship—to God, to creation, and, in consequence, to ourselves—there can be no true life for our souls, nor can there be any perfection.

The First Word *"Father, forgive them, they know not what they do."* (Luke 23:34)

The scene before us is terrible and excruciating.

Upon the Cross is our tormented, wracked, and dying Lord. It would seem that all is finished. Rage, revulsion, and hatred coming from His fellow men have caused Him to be entirely spent upon the Cross, from whence He shall not descend.

But what has He done to cause this rage, this hatred, and revulsion? He went about the land doing good. He healed the sick. He taught. He spoke so that His inspired listeners said, *"Never did man speak like this man"* (John 7:46). He set such holiness of life before their gaze that He alone among the children of men could ask: *"Which of you shall convict me of sin?"* (John 8:46). What caused this complete and terrible transformation of the minds and hearts of men? Strangely, each time a ray of His Divinity was seen through His Holy Humanity and each time He placed the seal of obligation, duty, and eternity upon all His words,[2] rage, hatred, and revulsion arose like waves in men's hearts. It was then that they took up stones with

2   *"Heaven and earth shall pass away, but my word shall not pass away"* (Mark 13:31).—The Author.

trembling hands. A single common emotion stifled their humanity: *"We desire Him not. We will not have Him to reign over us."*[3]

And when He at last definitively declared Himself to be God, He placed all of His law as a binding obligation upon all mankind without exception. Once again the vice of pride and the sin of Satan were repeated upon the earth—the creation of God stood before God and denied Him. The soul refused to accept Him as He is. She preferred to select her own god for herself. In fact, she has preferred to set herself in the place of God. And again we witness the worst and most terrible of sins.

When He declared that heaven and earth shall pass away, that His words shall not pass away, and that He is God, then everything changed. All of His words took on the character of obligations. They need not only be accepted, but made real at the cost of any sacrifice. And the soul replied: "I desire not to serve! I shall not! I do not submit!" As hatred, rage, and revulsion arose, she sought to trample upon and to obliterate God, a living and constant

3   Cf. Luke 19:14.—The Editor.

reproach. And how did God, made human flesh to save, purify, and raise this soul unto the divine life, reply to her? To her who persecuted her Incarnate God unto His final breath upon the Cross?[4]

In His testament from the Cross, Our Lord established the law for our relations to our fellow creatures: *"Father, forgive them, for they know what they do"* (Luke 23:34). In our day, too, when over and over again terrible sins are committed, the voice of the Lamb of God still resounds, proclaiming once and for all time: *"Father, forgive them, for they know not what they do."* Herein we find the explanation for God's forbearance. Accept that after Golgotha His shall no longer be a single voice. Unto His voice are added a choir of the souls who have accepted, nurtured, and made their own His law for our relation to creatures, proclaimed by Him, by their Lord, from His Cross: *"Father, forgive them, for they know not what they do."*

---

4   As our tormented, wracked, and downtrodden God cast His gaze down from the height of the Cross, He saw before Himself the rebellion of His creatures, a churning sea of rage, hatred, and revulsion.—The Author.

Our relationship to the created is the central question for the life of our souls. Without it there can be no proper relationship to God. This is the foundation upon which the entire house of our souls is erected. For our nature, wounded as she is by original sin, the question of our relationship to our fellow works of God is both a temptation and a stone of contradiction.

Our relationship to God is different now. Every religious soul is drawn unto God; she is impelled towards Him, at times even against her will. God is so wonderful and so generous that each genuine impulse toward Him is answered by an outpouring of grace. In this way, the soul is drawn ever more toward God, seeking to enter into the closest contact with Him. With fellow creatures, we have different relationships. We may be attracted to them, immersed in them, and seeking our own pleasure and satisfaction. This is the Pagan manner of relationship. Or else we may be hostile; we hate them and see in them the reason for all our misfortunes. We are at war with them, yet at the same time completely dependent upon them. This form of relationship is at the animal level. Or else, coming into contact with our fellow creatures, we perceive that "They are completely evil," and we walk away from them. We consider ourselves far superior to the world around us, and consider it our duty to treat others with indifference and scorn. All these attitudes are Pagan and not Christian. When she stands face to face with her hostile fellow creatures the soul is in need of a prescribed course. This is a crucial moment in the life of her soul, one upon which may depend all of her future spiritual development. This course is given us from the Cross: *"Father, forgive them, for they know not what they do."* In conformity with these words, a Christian's mindset may be merely Christian, or may be elevated to the sacrificial, that is, to the monastic. A Christian attitude toward the surrounding world is characterized above all by an illuminated and penetrating vision beyond appearances and into reality. Besides, and this is deeply important, such a mindset is characterized by detachment from ourselves and by the ability to evaluate things independently of the self and of how they act upon us. This vision sees only one unchanging and eternal criterion: God and Christ's sacrificial offering upon Golgotha.

When the people rely upon such an unshakable foundation, they shall begin to see all things in a new light. Firstly, they are confronted by the fact that all creation *"groans."* Evil and sin are the only true misfortune, because, above all, they tear us apart from God, but also because they are an abnormal, hideous, and despondent state. They make men weak, ugly, and ridiculous, but above all despondent. And, therefore, in place of all this rage and hatred for our hostile fellow creatures, the Christian must engender and develop feelings of pity and mercy towards them.

We must feel pity because the Christian needs to be aware that evil is both darkness and blindness of the soul. How can the soul not pity a fellow creature who unknowingly, or even worse, knowingly fails to see the Sun of Truth and Love, Who is our Lord Jesus Christ?

She must also feel mercy, because this pity shall create in the Christian a new, forgiving, and merciful heart. Grounded upon her new heart shall spring up goodwill, that is to say, the desire for the good and a willingness to repay with good the evil done by this dark, hostile, but deeply unhappy fellow creature. Surely, the greatest good is peace with God and His forgiveness. Henceforth, whenever we come into contact with a hostile fellow creature the prayer without ceasing of the Christian shall always be united with Jesus Christ's cry for mercy upon the Cross. It shall sound forever, withholding the avenging Right Hand of God and covering the sinner with a mantle of mercy: *"Father, forgive him."* How and from whence shall we find the reason for God's forgiveness?

All this may seem terrible upon the surface, but the Christian has learned through experience that only grace shall impart both knowledge of God and the necessary light and recognition to avoid sin. Therefore, in the blindness, darkness, and absence of the necessary recognition on the part of the hostile fellow creation, the Christian perceives the reason for forbearance and forgiveness—*"they know not what they do."*

Mercy engenders a desire for their good and a goodwill which is nothing less than the beginnings of love. The result is a compassionate stance toward the movements in the souls of others, a recognition of the mystery contained in another's inner life, and a respect for that mystery.

From all this there follows practical real-
ization of another great law of Christ—*"Judge
not."* The right to judge is not given you, for
the inner lives of your fellow creatures are a
mystery open to God alone, and to Him alone
belongs the right to judge. The Christian is
bound by the law of Christ: good is to be returned for evil; judgment and remission belong
exclusively to God—*"Father, forgive them, for
they know not what they do."* Yet there exists
an even higher stance regarding the hostile fellow creature: a sacrificial or monastic stance.
Nuns are especially called to partake of the
Lord's victory upon the Cross, and by this vocation they are summoned to Him. This entails
an awareness of our own personal responsibility and sinfulness. This is rooted in the Christian's attitude toward her fellow creatures, and
deeply suffused with the awareness of the
blindness and darkness within which the majority of people live who are apart from God—
"they know not what they do." Thus the soul is
filled with a different awareness: they do not
know. She knows, or at least she should know,
is required to know, and has been given everything necessary to realize this. From this flows

an awareness of her own responsibility before God and before the whole world for the least deviation from the path of truth. There shall also flow a deep awareness of our inadequacy and sinfulness, a sober severity toward herself, a merciful toleration for others, sorrow, strong acts of asceticism, and a thirst to be purified swiftly. On the basis of such an exalted and wonderful state there shall grow two dispositions which embrace the soul in her entirety. In their essence, they are a sacrificial and a co-redemptive disposition.

Above all, she shall possess a lively, deep sense of suffering with her fellow creatures and a fervent wish that *"they shall know and cease to do."* She shall also possess a desire by means of her personal, voluntary, and sacrificial acts in union with the Sacrifice of Golgotha to gain for them the worthiness for the pardon of the Father. This first disposition, however, does not attain its full measure without the second: which is a deep gratitude for the patience of the Lord Jesus Christ. He upends all her opinions, opens to her the light that grants true life—a co-redemptive love and a thirst together with His Own. Out of a pure love for Him, she shall stretch out her arms, pierced and crucified together with His, over the entire world. She shall then repeat without ceasing, in her words, in her life, and, as a nun prays less with her words than through who she is, chiefly by her person: *"Father, forgive them, for they know not what they do."*

The Second Word "Amen I say to thee, this day thou shalt be with me in paradise." (Luke 23:43)

The thief says, *"We indeed (are sentenced) justly, for we receive the due reward of our deeds; but this man hath done no evil"* (Luke 23:41). *And he said to Jesus, "Lord, remember me when thou shalt come into thy kingdom." And Jesus said, "... Amen I say to thee, this day thou shalt be with me in paradise"* (Luke 23:42–43).

A relationship with God has two basic characteristics. At the first there is a selfless recognition of the Tsar-like power of God, His authority over all things, and a proper attitude toward fellow creations of God. These may be seen in the words of the thief, and then in the reply of Christ, which reveals to us the mysteries of His Most Holy Heart.

We see in the words of the thief a very high degree of awareness: he has been sentenced justly and accepts the due reward of his deeds. This represents a very high level of thought. Yet we stubbornly refuse to acknowledge ourselves as guilty and worthy of everything unhealthy which we suffer at the hands of our fellow creatures. This is a constant deterrent on our path toward establishing a proper relationship of the self to God and His creations. We are actually transgressors of the law, and we should acknowledge this. In relation to the Graces poured out upon us from the Cross, the Chalice, and each of the Wounds of Jesus, we are offenders every hour and every minute, aiming constant blows at the Heart of Christ.

From such a sober and healthy recognition of our own sinfulness, a real desire flows for purification and a cry that all creation become a tool in the Merciful Hands of God to help us *"receive the due reward of our deeds."* And our deeds? It is profitable to recall them in those moments when all of our nature seethes, when a stifled outcry comes roiling up from the depths, when we rail against the situation we face, and against how we are treated. It is useful

then to unite ourselves with the Good Thief upon his cross and like him to imagine ourselves overwhelmed by tears of repentance unknown till now as our sinful life passes before us. For us, too, at such times we do well to recall our past deeds and perhaps our present ones as well. There is absolutely no doubt that each of us has in her life something similar. This something should awaken us to a sincere recognition together with the thief that in our dealings with our fellow creatures, *"We indeed (are sentenced) justly, for we receive the due reward of our deeds."* This takes a profound and exalted awareness of our sinfulness, a thirst for purification, and leads to a high degree of humility marked by a loving acceptance of insults and even gratitude for them.

"But He hath done no evil!" Here may be seen the ability to see and to place a proper value upon someone else's virtues. He has recognized Christ's Divinity through His wounded Humanity. *"Lord, remember me when thou shalt come into thy kingdom"* (Luke 23:42). This ability to see virtue in others, to value it, and to be glad of it is a beautiful, noble trait in the soul, but it is, unfortunately, a very rare one.

The Saints possessed this wonderful ability to a very high degree, extending it to all mankind. This displays a high ideal of the soul's relations with fellow creatures, and is based entirely upon good sense and upon what follows logically. Truly, if the soul is humble and wishes to search, she may find in any living creature virtues superior to her own. One is more obedient, another is more honorable, a third is more humble, a fourth is friendlier, and so on. Her ability to see the superiority of others evokes, on the one hand, a proper respect for creatures and helps her to struggle against temptations arising within. At the same time this automatically places the soul in the properly selfless and humble state of dependence upon her Maker. The good thief has gone to the very bottom of his own nothingness, has measured the bottomless pit of his sinfulness. In accepting that which according to his deeds is his *"due reward,"*[5] he ascended afterwards by way of the wounded Humanity of Christ to the heights of knowledge of Christ's Divinity. Now

---

5   Namely, condemnation and crucifixion at the hands of his fellow creatures.—The Author.

he is there before the face of his God in just the position which enables him to carry out an act of total self-giving and of perfect love. From his lips is torn a prayer, one of the most beautiful prayers ever to have poured out from the human heart: *"Lord, remember me when thou shalt come into thy kingdom."*

In order to attain holiness, the soul needs a selfless awareness of the Sovereignty and Tsardom of God, to take great joy in His glory, to not make her own demands, and to possess the ability to be content with little. *"He is the One Lord and Tsar of All, Whose glory is everywhere and fillest All Things[6]; I am nothing."* Truly, the good thief does not ask anything for himself. Forgiveness? He may well even think, given his own impudence, that this is not even possible. Really, in general, it is not of himself that he is thinking. He is looking upon Christ Crucified, and by the light of the Wounds of Christ he seems insignificant to himself. He agrees to all the torments of Purgatory until the end of time. One thing alone he thirsts for: that

---

6   An allusion to the Eastern Christian Prayer to the Holy Ghost, *"O Heavenly King."*—The Editor.

the Lord shall remember him, and only remember him. Undoubtedly to be remembered by God is salvation, but he is no longer thinking of himself. *"Lord, remember me!"* At this his thoughts of himself end, since another picture has unfolded before him. It engulfs him entirely, making him lose consciousness, making it possible and easy to bear all the torment of crucifixion and of Purgatory, which he willingly accepts.

Through Christ's wounded Humanity he has been brought to knowledge of Christ's Divinity. He no longer sees Christ debased and tormented upon the Cross of His own voluntary suffering. He sees Him as Tsar and Lord of the Universe, to whom all things are submitted without limitation. He reigns over all things and all creatures. They belong completely and undividedly to Him. It makes no difference whether the creature is willing to recognize this or not. And what pathetic mindlessness and blindness this is, to rebel against the sovereignty of the Good and the Merciful? For He is a Sovereignty who frees His creations from pathetic slavery to the created world and elevates them into a new, supernatural order of existence. The thief now sees Christ no longer in torment, immobile, nailed to His Cross, but rather free, shining with the glory of His Resurrection, in glory, at the right hand of His Father in the Kingdom of the Blessed. And he takes delight in the joyful contemplation of the infinite glory of His Lord and God. What triumph resounds in the wonderful words: *"When Thou shalt come into Thy Kingdom. Remember me, Lord, when Thou shalt come into Thy kingdom."*[7]

This is an exalted acknowledgement of the Tsar-like Power of Jesus Christ—crucified, humiliated, and tormented. To this amazing victory of the soul over the flesh and of the invisible over the visible, of the supernatural over the natural, and of grace over nature follows Christ's truly Tsar-like reply: *"This day thou shalt be with Me in Paradise!"* His reply is filled with such Tsar-like bounty! One opposite the Other, each crucified: one finds sufficient moral courage in himself that, ignoring himself, ignoring the created world, he fixes his

7   In the Byzantine Liturgy, these words proceed the chanting of the Beatitudes.—The Editor.

gaze upon Christ. He is transported to the heights of unity, proclaiming Jesus his only Lord, his God. The Other, from the height of His throne upon the Cross, making it known that the union of the purified creature with his God has come to pass: *"This day (and forever) thou shalt be with Me in Paradise. Not tomorrow, nor after some years of purification. Now. Today. At once. Thou hast acknowledged Me as thy Tsar and Lord, and I summon thee to dwell in My court. Where I shall be, thou shalt be with Me. Thou shalt be My companion for all time. Thou hast surrendered thyself and in thy humility asked only that I remember thee. And I give thee all, I give thee Myself, and I bear thee with Me forever. This day thou shalt be with Me in Paradise."*

This is the Holy Heart of Jesus, setting no limitations to His bounty. He pours Himself out completely, and in His immeasurable love He grants what is most valuable and most precious: Himself and for all time. *"This day thou shalt be with Me in Paradise."* What does this reply of Christ teach us: *"This day thou shalt be with Me in Paradise"*? He teaches us generosity in giving immediately of ourselves, which cannot be put off. The summons comes and the soul answers "Today." This is so hard for us, given our nature: "Tomorrow. I'll wait a while. I'll see …" No, not tomorrow. Today. At once. Right now. Each step taken in our direction we must return a hundredfold. The generosity of Christ and of His Most Holy Heart are the measure of our love.

"Thou shalt be with Me"! Let us wish that everyone may share in our spiritual blessings. Let us thirst to pour out upon everyone the gifts we have received. Let us share with all the life in Christ, with a generous and humble surrender of ourselves—*"This day thou shalt be with me in paradise."* Here upon the earth, in the enclosed garden of her secret life in Christ, the soul surrenders that she may be granted the eternal sight and possession of heaven. She thirsts for all, in the heavens and upon the earth, to commune with Christ. She thirsts for a readiness within everyone to accept any sacrifice, even death upon the Cross, if only to hear for themselves and for others this generous and Tsar-like promise of the Most Holy Heart: *"This day thou shalt be with Me in Paradise!"*

The Third Word "Woman, behold thy son …
behold thy mother." (John 19:26–27)

The moment of death, whether factually or
mystically, is the moment all our natural and
spiritual life progresses unto. As we contemplate the Crucifixion, we must always recall
that we see not merely Our Savior redeeming
us upon the wood of His Cross from our sins.
We also see the model in the life of our souls
and our Teacher of the paths to God: purification, illumination, and unification. It is as
though Our Lord placed His Crucifixion into
our hands and said: *"Behold and learn. Herein
lieth all wisdom."* Henceforth, we must always
approach His Crucifixion with this model in
our minds. In uplifting us upon the Cross with
Him, Christ leads us down a defined road of
Crucifixion and mystical death, beyond which
commences our true life in union with Him. In
His wounded wide-open arms, bowed head,
pierced feet, and pierced Heart, Christ truly is
our very life itself, in the deepest and fullest
sense of the term. In looking upon the Lamb
who was Slain we should say to ourselves,
*"Behold the source and the fullness of the life
of our souls. There is only in Him and through*

Him. There is no other way. Through the Wounds of His Humanity we ascend to knowledge of His Divinity."

Christ hung upon His Cross in all its terrible and tortured immobility. He was weary as during His earthly life and possessed no place to lay His Head. The agitation of the hostile crowd surrounded Him. He forgave them, teaching us the proper attitude toward creatures in rebellion. By His simple gaze and by the Graces pouring from his open wounds He summoned repentance in the heart of the thief, aiding him through selflessness, humility, and recognition of his total dependence upon God to uplift himself to unity with His Most Holy Heart. His heavy, tormented Head hung still lower and He saw She who was dearest to Him in the entire world, His Mother. She alone had always understood Him, She alone was able to grant Him the respect due to Him. She also had never in any way grieved His Most Holy Heart. Finally, She was able humbly to fall back and to hold herself in the shadows, never hindering His holy and sacrificial service in any way. She belongs entirely to the Father and to Him, a most holy, most pure creature, and a chosen vessel of grace.

Beside Her stood John, the young and wonderful flower of the love of Christ. He had given all his youth and his chastity to Jesus, and the Lord was truly able to look upon him with pleasure, for His own Most Holy Heart was reflected in the transparent purity of the heart of John. As nothing in them was repellent to Him these two created beings, Mary and John, evoked in Christ feelings of tenderness and great fondness. Just the opposite—their spotless purity harmonized with and echoed the Pure Humanity of Christ, and of His Holy Heart. At this crucial turning point, however, when everything in Christ's Humanity was hastening toward God alone, He gave us His last great teaching about renunciation of the created. This teaching is so important that before we speak of it we should announce: *"He that hath ears to hear, hear!"*[8]

Into the life of every soul that has chosen the decision to attain complete purification any and all cost and thus to open the way for God's action within herself,[9] there comes a turning

8   Cf. Matthew 11:15.—The Editor.
9   Meaning the firm and unshakable decision to do all

point—the time of great renunciation. At first this means a renunciation of the self, then renunciation of the most cherished and dearest being to which the soul may be attached in the noblest manner. This may even be he who led her to God. Taking pleasure and joy in the hold this being had over her, the soul herself ascended to God, praising Him and giving thanks. But she loved just this creature and no other. It was good to be together, and some very indefinable, very fine, and hardly noticeable thread held her attached to him and to no other.

The soul spent a long time persuading herself that she was ready to sacrifice this creature for God's sake and was ready to surrender him. Yet this attachment really did not hinder her movement toward God, but rather furthered it. To be with this creature evoked joy within her soul, the wish to speak of God, and to serve Him. Yet suddenly and not entirely comprehensible even to herself, a disquiet commences within the soul. An inner voice, the voice of Grace, firmly and insistently speaks to her and

she is able on her part and to leave the rest to God.—
The Author.

at times deprives her of peace, that she is still not completely free. This is still an attachment, although a very exalted one. God alone must reign. No one and nothing must reign with Him. There is only God for those who desire to journey to the mystical death of the Cross and the Wounds of Christ to Resurrection unto the blessed life of unity. God is Undivided Unity, and He never tolerates the least division or separation in the souls He has chosen for His Own. The attainment of this represents a high degree of purification. The soul completes the last stage of turning her whole self toward God, with no glance backward or to the side and with a complete detachment from what is very fine, very exalted, but nevertheless earthly, finite, and created. There is naught except God.

How many have come to this turning point in the life of their souls, to the final renunciation of the dearest, closest, and most beloved being? To him whose spiritual rebirth and growth they have perhaps given so much strength that he has become their favorite child? They feel no, it is impossible, and say to God: "Just not this, Lord. Some other time … Later …" But an irrepressible voice inside them stubbornly insists: "No, precisely this, and right now … There is naught except God."[10] Then, finally, with the help of His grace, we find sufficient strength within ourselves to carry out this final detachment from all created and finite things.

Lowering His head, Christ looked upon those who were the closest and the dearest to Him on earth and said: *"Woman, behold thy son,"* and *"Behold thy Mother."* He calls Her simply *"woman,"* one among many. With Her understanding soul She grasped everything. Easily and quickly, She accepted it. Making immediate reply to His new invitation of grace, she ascended to new heights of humility and renunciation. It is as though He is no longer Her Son, as though He has already left Her. Before Her now He is the great, terrible, and universal sacrifice. He is Her suffering and dying God. She stands to offer a new sacrifice. She is Virgin and Priest. She stands to offer the sacrifice

10 In the life of the soul, we must fear self-deception most of all, and we must ask God to evoke in us a holy disquiet, and to insistently repeat to us what it is He desires.—The Author

of the New Testament unto God the Father for all men and all creation. Through the Wounds of His Humanity, She reaches knowledge of His Divinity in a special and deeper sense. No one else among mankind possesses such reach to the Divine. For Her the Cross and the Pierced Lamb upon it constitute all knowledge and all wisdom and She, contemplating them, gains even greater love and even greater supernatural merit.

Yet Her Son is no longer present, although She receives His expired remains into Her Most Pure arms. She sees Him placed in the new tomb in Joseph of Arimathea's garden, wherein He shall lie in secret repose until the moment when, with the dawn of the Third Day, He shall arise in glory. She shall watch in Otherworldly joy as He, as conqueror of death and evil, ascends to Heaven in the Uncreated Light of the Eternal Glory, where He shall sit at the Right Hand of the Father. She shall then return home to wait, in constant works of charity, for the moment when She shall be forever reunited with Her Lord. All Her life, as the life of the Co-Redemptrix, has been self-denial without ceasing, up to that final great detachment upon

Golgotha. Then, instead of the Son whom She so loved and whose humanity was the breath of life to Her, She saw before Her eyes the great and terrible Sacrifice of the New Law.

If the soul truly enters into this mystery of purification and the emptying of all that is finite, earthly, and of even the most lawful and exalted attachments, her heart is involuntarily wrenched and feels terror before a tremendous emptiness. We know, in theory, that all must be brought to fulfillment by God and that in Him alone is our peace and our joy. Yet, practically speaking, we still feel that this is a desolation and an abyss, yet the Lord, as always, comes to meet us and prepares the way before us: *"Woman,"* he says, *"behold thy son."* And with these words He reveals to us the newly illumined and sanctified emotions which have come through the piercing of His Most Holy Heart.

This mindset toward creatures of God comes after full detachment from them, when the soul's purified and illumined gaze can look upon her neighbor with complete dispassion and objectively. It also comes when the soul draws all the motivation for her acts toward other created ones solely inside the Most Holy Heart of Jesus and without any influence of her own. Such a state of soul gains its best expression in the words "Maiden-Mother." It is as though Her Soul, having reached a state of complete detachment, truly accepted from Christ upon Golgotha His love and His Divine Feelings unto the created world. *"Son, behold thy Mother, Mother behold thy son."* This is the Maiden-Motherhood which makes the needs of all mankind Her own. She truly adopts all souls and bears them within Herself. Her Maternity has gained its most perfect expression in the Most Pure Heart of Mary. Her Maiden-Maternity, whose purity and exaltation may worthily be praised only by the choirs of angels, is inseparable from the soul of every nun. It is especially inseparable from she who understands her vocation properly and concentrates all her physical and spiritual strength upon fulfilling completely in her life unto the very end. Through her three vows, most especially that of obedience unto death upon the Cross, the soul has merited the right to stand at His Cross and to receive the last legacy of Christ. Unto One like Himself was entrusted the continuation of His work toward the salvation of mankind: *"Behold thy son. Behold thy Mother."*

What we see here is that the great gift of adoption as sons of God has been extended to the world entire. This moment of total renunciation fills us not only with terror and with a sense of emptiness, but also with Great Solitude. Our Lord knows that He must leave us for a time, and that we shall be confronted with a turning point in our spiritual lives with only the guidance we have already received. The Lord now turns his gaze to John. He knows that the pure heart of His disciple will be rent. In Christ John had everything—father, mother, friend, teacher, and the most wonderful among the sons of men. He was used to taking pleasure in Him and in His company, for both brought him the greatest joy. He loved Him not merely as God, but also as Man. In Jesus was all his joy. And now, at the foot of the Cross, what great loneliness he feels … The Lord looks upon him and says: *"Behold thy Mother. Behold Her in whose Most Pure Heart thou shalt find true support. She shall aid in uplifting thee unto a new companionship with thy Lord and God, wherein God alone shall reign."*

Strong and free, John descended from Golgotha as a new man. The eagle shall henceforth be the proper symbol for him. But he has descended from Golgotha with Mary. The Most Holy Virgin is essential to the life of our souls. She is our constant helper. She takes us into Her arms. She leads us unto God firmly and without deviation. Strongly yet gently, with Her maternal hand, She pushes aside all obstacles. She shelters us beneath Her mantle from all dangers and all enemies. How able She is in Her motherly way to smooth all our difficulties! She knows how to gain for us through Her intercession the strength to face all our difficult decisions and to set them in motion. And Our Lord, Who knew all this, spoke from the height of His Cross at the moment of His greatest anguish: *"Behold thy Mother."*

The Fourth Word "My God, my God, why hast Thou forsaken me?"(Matthew 27:46)

Our Lord, having spoken His Last Word to His Mother, now strives with all His suffering Humanity toward His Father in Heaven. His torments, both physical and spiritual, have grown ceaselessly. The waves of shame, weariness, exhaustion, and of isolation from all things have continued unabated. As these waves rise higher, all earthly things recede and disappear from His horizon. God alone remains. All of Christ's Humanity seeks a support in God and strives to find peace in Him.[11] But there is only the impenetrable immobility fixing His Body unto the Cross and holding Him motionless. Only His tormented Head may now be raised and lowered. He finds no point of support or minimal relief. The low heavy, leaden, and relentless sky hangs over Him. All is silent, with only the noise and agitation of the created beings below. Yet they do not affect Him. What He needs is God. What He desires is God alone. Yet God is silent. Before, God always heard Him. Now He hears Him no longer. Before, He always answered Him. Now He answers Him no longer …

There is only a great and impenetrable darkness, filled with abandonment and isolation with no means of escape. Upon His Cross the Son of Man truly has no place to lay His

11 What the tormented Humanity of our Lord seeks is rest, peace, and stillness in God.—The Author.

Head. Then, in His great weariness, He utters His Fourth Word upon the Cross. This is the cry of the unhappy, suffering soul to God, of the soul who, nevertheless, has remained faithful, looking for and desiring nothing apart from God: *"My God, my God, why hast Thou forsaken me?"*

After the final renunciation of the created world, there comes a decisive time in the life of the soul. At times, the Lord does not bring the soul into it immediately. He grants her a time to prepare and fills her with joy with His presence. It is only afterward that He leads her into Great Solitude.[12]

---

12 We must keep always before our eyes that God desires our union with Him, and disposes everything else toward that goal. He is so careful of the individuality of each soul and so respects and values her, that He gives each soul what is necessary for her to achieve union with Him in the most direct and speedy manner. Each progression of the soul is like an artistic creation by God and a free act of creativity. There are periods in the life of each soul which almost have to be repeated, but they too play themselves out differently. For some souls they are constant over the course of several years and for others they alternate with experiences of another order. But we must both know and believe that God disposes

This period may proceed in different ways. Sometimes it unfolds over a long period with no break. At other times it alternates with periods of sweet closeness to God. God leads the majority of souls precisely by this last form of Great Solitude, which is broken at intervals. It is only the strong souls that God sets upon the path of full abandonment over a long period of time. It is a courageous and thorn-strewn, but very true path. The state of these souls resembles that of the Human Soul of Our Lord Jesus Christ at the moment when He cried out to His Father: *"My God, my God, why hast Thou forsaken me?"*

Usually it is immediately after her renunciation of the created world that God places the strong soul upon the path of complete abandonment and Great Solitude. Sometimes, however,

everything for the benefit of each soul. Thus, the period of growth which I call Great Solitude—which could not be more apposite to the Fourth Word of our Lord—is repeated in the life of almost every soul precisely because it is absolutely essential for our moving ahead. It is like a touchstone of the goodwill, sincerity, and righteousness of the soul. It shows how willing she actually is to renounce everything and to bear all things for the sake of glorifying God and uniting herself to Him.—The Author.

He first grants the soul a glimmering of the joy
of union with Him. Once this happens the soul
is finished with the world and no longer finds
within it anything that is at all attractive. Even
what is dearest and closest seems to recede
from her view: something further is needed.
The soul understands with all her being that her
point of support is in God. He is more necessary to her than anything upon the earth, because all that is created and finite is now distant
from her. The soul turns toward God with all
her naked, tormented, and wounded being. And
she is met by a complete and grave-like silence.
The heavens are closed. It is as though the soul
hung suspended on air and completely alone.
The material world beneath her seems unreal,
transparent, and above all unnecessary and
pointless. And there is nothing above her except a low and leaden sky. This is more than
emptiness. It is like to an airless expanse or,
more precisely, the immobility of being nailed
to the Cross after the torments are done. Then
a dull and exhausted weariness comes and also
a sharp awareness that there is nowhere to lay
her head. And He for Whom the soul abandoned everything is silent. All that remains for

the soul is to raise her gaze unto the closed heavens, with the unshakable hope uniting herself to the Pierced Lamb upon the Cross and to stubbornly repeat his cry: *"My God, my God, why hast Thou forsaken me?"*

Two basic traits characterize this time when the soul is ascending toward God. There is a sense of total abandonment and awareness of her total isolation and emptiness which only God can fill.[13] The characteristics of this state are:

1) Weariness and regret toward the world, sometimes to the point of utter revulsion. The temptation is to leave everything and to avoid contact with fellow beings. The soul must resist courageously, laboring to gain for herself the necessary disposition and patience to

---

13 Great Solitude is an extremely important and significant time for the development of the soul who endures it. It is a crucial moment in the life of every soul, for this time is precisely what refines the gold and constructs the fortress necessary to contain the Presence of her Lord and God, Who shall follow. Great Solitude shall also consume the straw of the sensual and emotional life within her.—The Author.

carry out her obligations unswervingly and as blamelessly as possible. She must do this no matter how tiresome and agonizing these obligations become.

2) A great longing for support and a temptation to seek this support from fellow creatures, whereas even her spiritual father[14] and monastic superior cannot provide it. The soul has reached the moment when all of her support must be in God and in Him alone. Instruction and submission are more necessary to her than ever before. The soul must continue to open herself with both simplicity and childlike purity of heart. She must also follow unswervingly the counsel she receives. In the darkness which surrounds her, submission is the guiding lamp. Within herself there is no other light. She sees nothing, hears nothing, and understands nothing. She cannot find support, refuge, or consolation on earth and, therefore, she must withstand the tempta-

---

14 Among Eastern Christians, a primary tool of the spiritual life involves "submission to a spiritual father."—The Editor.

tion to discouragement and sorrow which weaken her. She must resist this with the awareness that her support and consolation must only be found in God. She must patiently wait for Him, and He shall come. This is what hope and obedience tell her. There is nothing else, except to call out with her Lord upon His Cross: *"My God, my God, why hast Thou forsaken me?"*

3) Only sorrow and weariness are drawn out of the soul's spiritual exercises and especially from oral prayer. How hard it is, even unbearable, to whisper with dried out lips words which seem to have lost all meaning, for it is as though no One is hearing them. Sometimes it is in prayer when the feelings of isolation and abandonment reach their most acute point, for this was the time when we met God and conversed with Him. When no One comes to us and no One answers, all that remains is to continue waiting and crying out without ceasing, *"My God, my God, why hast Thou forsaken me?"*

Once God does not answer and enliven every one of the works we do with His life-giving

Breath, spiritual reading also becomes torturous and loses all meaning. God, Heaven, and all things are dead. He remains silent. The temptation is to cut our spiritual exercises short and to think up some new physical task which will distract us from the constant weariness. The way to combat this is through working toward constancy, no matter what ensues, with a stubborn insistence on prayer. We must say with our whole being, in brave expectation: *"Lord, I am here. I await."* Dangerous temptations for the soul at such times are the following:

1) A desire to seek distraction and rest in tasks which we think up, perhaps at times very serious, important tasks, but which serve at the same time to distract the soul from the immobility and the weariness of Crucifixion. We may also think of works that might at times be very serious and important, but which are motivated, all the same, by the desire to descend from the Cross.

2) The temptation to disobedience against our superiors, which does not satisfy or provide the comfort sought by the tormented soul, but, on the contrary, makes her sense of

abandonment and the reality of her isolation all the more acute. The soul must also
resist the tendency to criticize and to avoid
her superiors, and to lock herself up inside
herself.

3) The hardest and most dangerous temptation is against hope: *"If this continues, I
shall be unable to withstand it."* However,
the faithful soul shall stand fast and shall
inspire the choirs of angels with her hero-
ism. She shall have the help of the grace—
unseen and un-sensed—which pours out
upon her from the Wounds of Christ, Who
bore these same torments before the soul
and for her sake.

There is another manner of temptation
against hope: awareness of the inescapability
of the situation. *"Heaven is closed, God is
silent, and the dull, gray days stretch forward
as though I have been abandoned in a cold and
dark cellar. Over there is light, and the birds
are singing. In general there is a completely
different life than here, but all of that is not for
me. I am condemned for all my days to a with-
ering without God, without the sun, and without*

joy. Beyond the grave there is Purgatory stretching on and on. Perhaps there is Hell. Perhaps I am already condemned and rejected by God, and this is Hell beginning on earth."

The soul must respond decisively and firmly that she is ready, out of love for her Crucified God, to suffer this way all her life.

The soul must develop patience, constancy, and an unshakable faith in her Lord and God. When she directs her eyes unto the Crucified Lamb of God and hears His cry: *"My God, my God, why hast thou forsaken me?"* she shall manfully and firmly pass by the road of isolation and abandonment. The length of this road is defined exclusively for her by the goodness and love of God. Then, within the soul wonderful fruits shall mature by the action of Grace. These fruits shall make her capable of further ascent toward the heights of the life of our souls.

These fruits are:

1) A deep awareness of the truth of St. Francis of Assisi's words: *"My God is all that's mine."* In the One God is all our support and all the life of our souls;

2) The ability to look upon all things with the

eyes of faith and to hope in God despite appearances and all that seems evident;

3) Freedom and independence from sensuality and emotion;

4) The ability to master herself, in both external appearance and within;

5) And finally, the most wonderful of the fruits, a deep internal peace; a peace of soul that does not depend upon events in the external or internal world. The soul shall then be ready to go on to additional works and to receive the Graces sent by God.

What consolation this is to the souls who pass along this difficult road of abandonment and complete isolation! God loves them greatly. He both sees and cares for them. Together with them He relives His abandonment upon Golgotha and sees in them the embodiment of His cry: *"My God, my God, why hast Thou forsaken me?"* God looks with love upon them and awaits the time when He shall come with His love to reward them for their fidelity, patience, and constancy. Yet these souls must remember that they must bear their abandonment and loneliness in the closest unity with the sufferings of Jesus Christ upon the Cross. They must never let the Crucifixion and Lamb Who was Slain upon His Cross escape from their view. They must cry out with all their being and without ceasing: *"My God, My God! Why hast thou forsaken me?"*... And await their time ... And the Lord shall come.

The Fifth Word "I thirst." (John 19:28)

Our Lord Jesus Christ has now experienced all the weariness of abandonment and isolation expressed in His cry to the Father: *"My God, my God, why hast thou forsaken me?"* He gave over His Holy Humanity to a new emotion that flowed directly from awareness of abandonment by God and of the need for Him. The Holy Soul of the dying Man-God filled to overflowing with the desire expressed so clearly and strongly by the words *"I thirst."*

For what did the Most Holy Heart of Jesus so thirst? He thirsted first of all for Unity with God His Father in Heaven and the full completion of His great sacrificial offering, as would be accomplished on the day of His Most Glorious Ascension. Jesus thirsted for that for which He had prayed: *"Father, the hour is come.*

Glorify Thy Son that Thy Son may glorify Thee" (John 17:1). This He expressed in a mysterious way through His words to Mary Magdalene: *"Do not touch me, for I am not yet ascended to My Father"* (John 20:17). His thirst was to go to His Father and complete His Great Work of the glorifying His Father by means of the One Victim of the New Testament worthy in His sight. This desire filled the Most Holy Heart of Jesus as He cried out: *"I thirst."*

His Heart desired the glorification of His Father here on earth as well: *"... Thy kingdom come, Thy will be done!"* (Matthew 6:9). All of the Holy Humanity of Our Lord desired that the greater glory of God be made known and manifest. With a great longing, Jesus longed for the fruits of His Redemptive Act for men's souls. He longed for the salvation of souls and for the conversion of as many souls as possible. He longed for perfected and self-sacrificing souls whose own objective is to achieve the joy of working with Him, regardless of all obstacles, for the Redemption. Above all, He desired sacrificial souls who, like to Him, shall voluntarily nail themselves upon a Cross and make the firm and unshakable decision that they shall not descend even if all the world, their own flesh, and even their own reason cry out without ceasing: *"Descend from thy Cross and we shall believe! Thou wilt save the world entire, only come down from thy Cross, for this is unbearable not merely for thee, but for us as well!"* And Our Lord knew and saw that there would be souls like to these, who shall not descend from their Cross even if their poor and tormented nature should beg, *"Grant me a minute's rest! Descend from thy Cross just for the hour! Descend now!"* No, there is no rest nor term to the Cross. It is to the end and it was for such souls which the Most Holy Heart of Jesus longed when He cried out, *"I thirst"* in His Agony upon the Cross. During His Passion these souls, first of Whom was His Most Pure Maiden-Mother, were the consolation and joy of His Heart.

We must set ourselves courageously and decisively before Him and hear His cry, *"I thirst."* By an act of our wills we must forge an awareness of that within us which the Most Holy Heart so thirsted for. Christ thirsted for us not as we are, but for the sacrificial ideal of us that He bore, aflame with love and desire, within His Heart. The soul feels all the sufferings of abandonment and isolation. By an act of the will, she has remained faithful to her Lord and God. She has affixed herself, taut as the string of a violin, unto her own Cross of abandonment. Humbly she has refused all that presented itself and has agreed to serve Christ in darkness and isolation. In consequence she has learned to value her Lord and God, to appreciate the smallest sign of Attention from Him, and to recognize that, compared to Him, all else is nothingness and is valueless.

Gradually the soul begins to recognize the stirring of a new life within herself; abandonment, isolation, awareness of God's Presence, and finally an unquenchable and burning desire for Him. Yes, first she desires, and then thirsts, for the Living God. *"Give me God,"* she asks unceasingly of everyone she encounters on her path. It truly is as though she were in constant motion, moving and sometimes running, and ever propelled by her unquenchable thirst. *"I desire my God and I seek Him without ceasing. Give me my God."* She truly could repeat the words, *"I thirst,"* without ceasing, morning and eventide, at prayer, at labor, and even in sleep.[15] All of her being is concentrated in a single desire: *"I desire God."*

Mary Magdalene says, *"Tell me where thou hast laid Him, and I will take Him away"* (John 20:15). The force of her desire is so strong that it is as though her desire has blinded her. It seems as though she sees nothing and does not recognize the Glorified Christ. In the force of her emotion, to her it seems that she is capable of doing anything: *"I will take Him away."* With these wonderful words *"I will take Him away,"* we pass over to the second basic trait characterizing the soul in this period. It is not enough to desire God, to seek after Him with all of her being, to look for Him everywhere and in everything, or to inquire about Him from everything and everyone. (*"Where hast thou laid Him?"*) The soul must also work for God.

---

15 Among Eastern Christians, the Biblical injunction to *"Pray without ceasing"* is taken to mean the mantra-like repetition of *"The Jesus Prayer."* As established by the first monks in fourth-century Egypt, the words *"Lord Jesus Christ, Son of God, have mercy on me, a sinner"* are chanted until similarly repeated mentally, during both waking and sleeping hours. It is to this that Mother Catherine is referring.—The Editor.

(*"I will take Him away."*) For Him she has already done a great deal, always doing her utmost, humbly submitting all her nature to Him, and constantly making herself obedient to the Holy Ghost. She has always done what she should, serving her neighbor and being obedient.

But now she senses a mysterious welling of strength within herself, a strength exceeding her nature. (*"I will take Him away."*) All that has been done up to now seems petty, pale, and paltry. She desires the arduous and the great. For the love of her Lord she desires the heroic and the valiant. She wishes to give herself totally in union with Her Crucified God, for He lives in her soul, and within her soul she constantly hears His final cry: *"I thirst."* She wishes to be obedient unto death, death upon a Cross. She winds a crown of thorns around her forehead. She opts for blind obedience, the higher part of her soul exalting, but with her human nature reacting with irritation. She carries out Acts of Humility that cause her whole nature to stand on end. The soul is filled entirely with joy and takes upon herself the hardest and most demeaning of tasks. She is glad when these tasks wear her body out. She wants only to labor for others and, even as her body repeatedly cries out in protest, she voluntarily takes upon herself mortification of the self. But somewhere within, not knowing wherein herself, some stubborn, insistent voice says: *"Go on. Forward, still farther. This is still too little."* Hair shirts, chains, and fasts, all become the object of the soul's desires. And all still seems insufficient for truly sharing in and quenching the *"I thirst"* of Christ.

The soul begins to thirst not merely to give all her blood drop by drop for Christ, but to pour it all out entirely. She desires martyrdom. This represents the end point of all her desire for herself. There is no way to proceed farther. Simultaneously, the more closely the soul makes Christ's thirst upon the Cross a part of her own life, the more deeply she enters into the desires of His Most Holy Heart, the more her own heart is broadened by a new thirst. Thus, a thirst for the salvation of souls appears. The love of Christ grants no rest to the soul. He rouses her to bring everyone to Christ, even those farthest from Him, those most alienated from Him, and those who are most hopeless.

This is the point upon which great missionary vocations are born. This is the time when, putting everything aside, people depart for distant lands to preach the Gospel of Salvation and, if possible, to gain a martyr's crown. Whole monastic communities have been born precisely from this thirst of our Lord Jesus Christ upon His Cross. Yet it is not enough to quench the thirst within the Heart of Christ or to burn with this same thirst. The soul feels very limited. It seems as though she cannot be sufficient and that it is not enough to individually share and to quench the thirst of Christ. She begins to thirst for zealous souls who shall make it an objective to quench the thirst of the Lamb of God for perfected spirits. And, in this direction, she begins to labor and to pray. In every way available, she tries to awaken within the souls of those that come to her a desire to follow after the Cross of Christ, to love the Cross, and take the Cross entirely upon themselves. *"I thirst not just for my own perfection, but for that of others. And, if I cannot quench the thirst of the Heart of Christ, then let others do so who are more ardent and more consequential, only let His thirst be quenched."* The advent of this moment of altruism is extremely important, for it shows the sincerity and the absence of self-interest in her *"thirst,"* as it is so well expressed in the words of the Lord's Prayer: *"Hallowed be Thy name." "And if not I then let others, and I am ready to serve them all my days."*

The greatest and most true virtue of the thirsting soul is zealousness. This appears in all places. It is a fervor for all that is most difficult for our nature. As a result the soul undertakes the most difficult tasks, joyfully accepting unpleasantness, with zealousness in her neighbor's service, and with a willingness to take upon herself all the sufferings and difficulties connected with service. The fruits of this state are to have labored for true zealousness and to be detached from her personal emotions. There is also suffering and having her foundation exclusively in a desire to assuage the thirst of the Most Holy Heart.

Yet this state also presents great risks of its own for the soul:

1) Excessive fervor in regard to herself, seeking to go beyond the boundaries of

obedience, and overestimation of her own strengths. This leads to criticism of her superiors and a notion that they do not understand the soul, hold her back, and fail to appreciate her.

2) The latter leads the soul to self-deception and pride, and an exaggerated notion of her spiritual accomplishments. Thus, in place of a moment of altruism, the soul reaches a moment of egotism. She excludes others, and gains a false notion that she has been chosen, and is greater and more exalted than others.

3) Excessive fervor in relation to others: a tendency to lead everyone down the soul's own path, applying pressure, and impatience with any opposition on their part, whether in the way they are treated or in the quest for their perfection.

From all this an extremely demanding treatment of others may follow. The end point of this improper course is love of power and impatience with any demonstration of independence on the part of our neighbor within their own spiritual life. Yet always remember that direction from and obedience to superiors are what bring the soul from the thorny pathways to the heights, and to guide her around each of these obstacles. It is necessary for the soul to always remember that, regardless of all these troubling things in our world, she must accept all things, laying them at the Pierced Feet of Our Lord. For the majority of souls, both Spiritual Thirst and Great Solitude repeat at intervals and alternate with other states; their meaning is therefore very important for our souls.

That is why, in conclusion, I shall impart to you two pieces of advice:

1) Do not attempt to stifle this thirst within yourself. To the contrary, endeavor to broaden and deepen it. Leave yourself, your own feelings, and your own trials aside. Make this thirst a supernatural one and unite it with Our Lord's Thirst upon His Cross.

2) Never decline Grace or the Promptings of Grace. God perceives both the soul's thirst and her desire to do something for Him. Very often, in coming Himself to help her, He prompts her toward decisions that run

contrary to her nature. Instead of making these decisions with obedience, the soul attempts under various pretexts to escape from them, or else, not being able to choose to refuse God directly, she does not immediately follow His Voice but rather delays for a time. Beware of such refusals: with but one such refusal the whole spiritual thirst may spend itself. Remember that there are no small matters in the life of our souls. Sometimes the Holy Heart asks merely some small and insignificant service. Under the pretext that this is a small matter which may be delayed and which is unimportant, you decline Him. Rather, we must strive to hear the Voice of Our Lord from the Height of His Cross and to assuage the thirst of His Most Holy Heart.

The Sixth Word "It is consumed." (John 19:30)

Suddenly, as She stood at the foot of His Cross contemplating the great Sacrifice of the New Testament, the Most Holy Virgin saw a new light in the eyes of Her Son and Her God. This light slowly suffused Christ's entire Face.

His agony was gone, His breathing again became full and unhindered, and His Crucified body suddenly straightened as though energized by some new emotion. He found the strength not merely to speak but to let forth a triumphant cry that terrified the soldier who stood at the watch. His cry resounded and ever shall as the cry of Tsar and Victor, *"It is consumed."* At this instant, Jesus leaves all sorrow, pain, and weariness behind forever. *"It is consumed."* God the Father has been glorified and in Christ He has received all the glory possible from a Creature. The damage inflicted upon the glory of God by all the sins of the world, starting with the Sin of Adam, have been more than fully expiated. Christ's mission is completed and needs no one and nothing more.

With the help of His Graces, His mercy, goodness, and love grant us the option of participating in His Act of Redemption and in the glorification of His Name. Within the Body of Christ, friendship between God and man has been reestablished. The battle without ceasing between the sin of the creature and the justice of the Creator, between depravity and the holiness of the Maker of souls, has ended. Salvation is opened to sinners and there is no longer any sin which may not be forgiven.

Yet that is not all. Christ's *"It is consumed"* does not merely open a simple friendship for us, but levels of friendship of which the angels could never dream. The soul, washed by the Holy Blood of Christ, may now go not merely from death to life, but, along various stages of this life, she may reach the perfection of sanctity. David could thirst for God and could strive to please Him. Yet, prior to the death of Christ, neither David nor anyone could attain the final hope of both Human and Divine desires. But now this desire is open to anyone who shall accept and willingly take upon herself the necessary sacrifices. By the strength of the Holy Blood and through the Graces from the Mysteries,[16] which are given us by its being shed, all actions, words, and thoughts may be brought unto obedience in Christ. Moreover, the soul may, with the help of these same Graces, reach such full unity of life with Him that she may

16 Among Eastern Christians, the Sacraments are always referred to as the Mysteries.—The Editor.

truly cry out, *"I live, now not I, but Christ liveth in me"* (Galatians 2:20).

"It is consumed." Christ's task is not completed in the sense of being immobile or closed. No, rather His task is accomplished similarly to a human body in a mother's womb, which shall be brought to a new life through suffering. The sufferings of Christ's Passion shall now reverberate within His Mystical Body and Mother Church shall undertake and complete what lacks in His sufferings. The Church shall join them with the soul not merely for her salvation but—principally—for her full attainment in the likeness of her Crucified Bridegroom. It is to these very souls that His last cry *"It is consumed"* hath been addressed.

Jesus knew that His Human Soul had rendered the fullness of glory unto His Father. In Him, the Name of His Father has attained the highest degree of His Glory, and now *"It is consumed."* All that now remains, *"And now glorify Thou Me, O Father, with Thyself, with the glory which I had, before the world was, with Thee"* (John 17:5). Furthermore, He saw the Tsar-like road opening for men's souls: the road to Golgotha, to mystical death, resplendent Resurrection, unity with Him, and eternal life in Heaven.

It is consumed! He saw the white-robed company forever surrounding the Lamb. They are the fruit of His *"It is consumed"* and of His victory over the world, the flesh, and the devil. He knew, of course, that in Him alone resides the fullness of God made Manifest. He knew that with His glorified Wounds, He is a completed masterpiece of extraordinary beauty. Yet, as St. Thomas[17] has said, the highest good must be everywhere extended. Even as the sun sends out her rays although she herself does not have need of them, the souls who follow Christ unto the end are the rays of the Sun that is Him. His *"It is consumed"* spoken from the height of His Cross is relevant to them, for through them the great task of Jesus, a task greater and more difficult than the Creation of the World, is brought to fruition.

Then God made out of nothing and nothing opposed His Word of Creation. *"For He spoke and they were made: He commanded and they*

17   Saint Thomas Aquinas.—The Editor.

were created" (Ps. 33:9).[18] *"And God said, 'Be light made'; and light was made"* (Gen. 1:3). What illumination, what freedom, and what quickness may be felt in this Act. Nothing is in opposition and the Act of Creation is the work of God's Omnipotent Power. Then the Son of God takes upon Himself the great work of the re-Creation of the created and cries, *"Behold, I come to do Thy will, O God."*[19] He must not merely commit violence against His Divinity by attiring Himself in human nature—*"A body Thou hast prepared for Me"*[20]; He shall also encounter a great obstacle along on the way to His Grace-filled and Merciful Act.[21] This obstacle is the soul's free will and also her dark and rebellious nature. But the primary obstacle is her free will. Everything is, after all, a question of the will, as restrained and directed by Grace.

---

18   In the Douay-Rheims Bible, upon which I have relied as often as possible, this verse appears as Psalms 32:9.—The Editor.
19   Hebrews 10:9.—The Editor.
20   Hebrews 10:5.—The Editor.
21   His Act is not merely the salvation of mankind, but the raising of each purified soul unto the level of marriage with Him.—The Author.

The Lord hath had to struggle against and conquer the most evil of man's enemies, His own ego. *"A man's enemies are those of his own household,"*[22] says Holy Scripture. Of those with whom he lives the closest and most dangerous is his own self. This is why the Redemption and Sanctification of mankind, which the Lord has taken upon Himself, is an act of pure and infinite love.

Draw profit from the two fruits of this Sixth Word from the Cross:

1) Learn to contemplate His *"It is consumed"* as the Glorification of God in Jesus Christ being brought to fruition. Thus you shall see Him, beautiful in His glorified wounds, as the *"fullness of the Sun of the Father's glory."* Do this so that all your being shall learn to be elated by His Beauty and to be triumphant with the Angels and Archangels, Thrones, Powers, Principalities and Dominions ever more frequently. Detach yourself from yourself and from all your surroundings: *"And I beheld, and I*

22 Matthew 10:36.—The Editor.

heard a voice of many angels round about the throne, and the living creatures and the ancients, and the number of them was thousands of thousands, saying with a loud voice, 'The Lamb that was slain is worthy to receive power and divinity and wisdom and strength and honor and glory and benediction'" (Apocalypse 5:11–12).

2) Let deep gratitude unto your Knight and Bridegroom, Our Lord Jesus Christ, fill you to overflowing. He has freed you from a cruel enemy, that is, from your own self. In the life of every soul who sincerely seeks and strives to glorify God through her perfection and is ready for His sake to make any sacrifice, there comes a great moment. The Lord leans downward from the Height of His Cross and says to the soul with inexpressible love: *"It is consumed. Thou art Mine. There is no returning. Everything hath left thee but Me. I am all that thou hast and outside of Me is nothing for thee. It is consumed."*

This extraordinary and special love may be granted to individual souls. Yet this is not granted in the natural order of things. Of herself, the soul hears nothing and thinks nothing. Yet she knows that something has taken place within her. She cannot exactly define when and, yet, she knows that there was a moment in her life before which she was one way and afterwards entirely different. Suddenly, everything that, in the realm of the spiritual life, had seemed unclear, confusing, incomprehensible, and upsetting became clear, obvious, simple, and logical. And this is why: peacefully and without any emotion an inner voice has spoken. An unusual division between the interior from the exterior has ensued. The Word of God is living and, more piercing than a two-edged sword, hath reached unto the division between the soul and the spirit.[23]

Above all, this state is characterized by illumination and by the proper discernment of the Word of God. The soul is fed in a special way by the Truths of the Faith. She does not even say, *"I believe."* Rather, she desires to say, *"I know that this so. I see it."* The illumination of God's Word truly pierces, like a two-edged

23   Cf. Hebrews IV;12.

sword, to her depths. This mysteriously divides the spirit from the flesh and her lower part, or spirit,[24] from the higher part, or soul.[25]

The soul strongly feels this division, like to a new light within herself. It truly is *"consumed."* There exists a new and purified inner gaze, which draws her to Eternal Truths and strives to build a foundation for her conduct within those truths. The clouds have been scattered that hid the soul's peak from view. The Lord has left that snowy-white and wonderful peak for Himself alone. It is true that the peak is not shining as yet, for the soul still must pass through the winter of silence that is Saturday in the Tomb. Yet she is there, present, purified, and ready to receive the rays of the Sun of Love. The Sun will come in His time, that is,

24   In the Russian language, two Old Slavonic words are used to describe the innermost self. The word Душа (Dusha), which is used here, refers to the emotions, the passions, and the thoughts which are guided by them.—The Editor.

25   The word Духа ("Dukha") refers to the intellect, the ability to listen, and the emotional equilibrium. When someone has become depressed or despondent, it is said in Russian that their "Dukha has fallen." —The Editor.

in the Lord's own time. But already *"It is consumed,"* and all things are prepared. The Sword of Christ hath brought about the division necessary to release the soul for a deeper interior relationship with her God. All this, perhaps, may seem obscure to all of you. Earlier perhaps, glimmerings of this division were present within the soul, but we now speak of a constant state. It is only to this state that *"It is consumed,"* the cry from the Cross, is directed.

1) The first basic characteristic is an extraordinary realism. At times, this even frightens the soul and exists to such a degree that the landscape of unseen realms and the Truths of the Faith appear sharply and well-defined. Equally well-defined are the transparency and unreality of all surrounding the soul and, above all, of her own temporal existence. Equally distinct is her awareness of eternity, of her vocation, and of her Betrothal to Christ. From this is drawn a holy indifference to all that proceeds around her, an indifference above all to her own person, and a complete independence from both people and circumstances. This holy liberty,

both internal and external, arrives regardless of total obedience. This conveys a great reverence to authority, which results from the reality of the Truths of the Faith.

2) Her own behavior is founded upon eternal truths. Henceforth, the carrying out of charitable works shall be both easy and comfortable. It is natural, easy, and simple for the soul to perceive God in her spiritual father and superiors and, accordingly, to show them a ready and calm obedience in both interior and exterior matters.

3) Objectivity: a complete freedom from all creatures and from all distractions arising from them. The soul takes, in addition, a sober and objective view of all things and of all mankind. She also takes a constant and detached view of herself and applies objective criteria. This conveys a serene clarity and the ability to see herself in an amusing light, with good-natured humor, and even with joyfulness.

4) In undertaking spiritual exercises, such a soul shall be ever more drawn toward standing motionless before God, toward receiving Light from Him, and toward

partaking of Him. A single word from a spoken prayer, Psalm, or piece of spiritual reading shall be enough for her to be nourished and given food for an entire day. This serves less for reflection than for being inwardly filled by the reality of the Divine. A mysterious light is revealed to the soul in all things and only the simplest words are needed for her nourishment. Complex constructs of thought cease to satisfy her. Merely the Sweet Name of Jesus, speaking from the Holy Scriptures, shall plunge her into motionless contemplation. The Mysteries and the Life of Divine Truths are opened before her: *"It is consumed."*

5) Freedom from temptations. Yes, they are still present, somewhere on the surface and far away. Yet the soul regards them as though she were a spectator, and sometimes smiles at herself and at her own pitiful nature. Most often she makes acts of humility and reacts to her temptations by paying close attention to them. As required, she pacifies and humbles herself to insure against even the least inclination to Pride. She always engages in acts directly

opposite to her temptations and recognizes that within herself, she has strong defenses which cannot be breached, because *"It is consumed."* The two-edged Sword of Christ has cleansed the peak of the soul. Other than His Grace, He shall not permit anyone or anything to enter in. The soul is both His fortress and His domain.

6) The last quality flows from those which preceded it: a tempered and unshakable fidelity within the soul to God the Father, to Christ her Bridegroom, and to all that represents God upon earth. First of all, this refers to the Church, Her Head, the soul's shepherds and teachers, and on to her direct superiors. This brings fidelity of thought and an independence from all things external, temporal, and perishable. She is based solely upon the invisible and eternal Truths of the Faith. This fidelity is removed from all things concrete and from all visible facts. She must have no criticism or judgments of the conduct and personality of those who bear their authority from God. There are neither standing nor grounds. This is simply irrelevant to the soul, as she

does not even see these matters and instead sees something entirely different. She sees the essential inner reasons for faith and God acting from the exterior. And hence comes, in consequence, the soul's liberty and an unshakable dedication to the interests of Christ, His Church, to her Order, and to the Superiors and representatives of that Order. Both in joy and in grief, she shall be their faithful and dispassionate fellow laborer. At all times and in all things, they may rely upon her. She shall not falter or waver, even if the whole world shall rise against her and all facts shall appear to contradict her. Our Lord may rely upon the soul. She is entirely His, one in substance, and undivided. *"It is consumed."* For her He is the One, True, and only God in existence. And she shall willingly accept martyrdom, exile, shame, and disgrace, not without emotion or sentiment, yet with unshakable fidelity. If this shall be the destiny set by God for the soul, she shall follow it through to the end. She shall not descend from the Cross. They shall only take her down dead. There remains but one further step, or rather a single and final breath, prior to complete mystical death. Then, a radiant Resurrection with the dawn of the Third Day shall lift the soul unto complete and joyful union with her Lord and God: *"It is consumed."*

The Seventh Word "Father, into Thy Hands I commend My Spirit." (Luke 23:46)

The time of Great Calm drew nigh. Our Lord knew that this was to be His final *"Night upon Earth,"* after which an everlasting cloudless day would come with the dawn of the Third Day. As His Most Pure Mother taught Him, He commended His soul unto God in the night before sleeping.[26] And now, upon this night most different from other nights, He commended His soul into the Hands of His Father: *"'Father, into Thy Hands I commend My spirit.' And, saying this, He gave up the ghost."* The evening of peace had come, and that Sabbath Day was approaching when His eyes should encompass all the works He had done. *"And God saw everything that He had made,*

26 Sleep being symbolic of death.—The Author.

and behold, it was very good. And it was evening ... And on the seventh day God finished His work which He had done, and He rested on the seventh day from all His work which He had done" (Genesis 1:31; 2:2).

Contemplation of the peace of death that Jesus Christ was entering into is one of the most fruitful things for the life of our souls and, tragically, we often set it aside. We know not how to remain with Christ during His mysterious repose in the Tomb. Reverence for Our Lord fallen asleep has never developed within us and we continue to forget Him. He worked for thirty-three years, from the time of His first breath in the cave at Bethlehem. He did not repose for a single minute. His Holy Heart was wakeful even in the night, for His work was a complete inversion of the entire world, both interior and exterior. No culture shall survive or advance if it be not in conformity with Him and with His law.

In order to live and remain forever among the people, He founded the Greatest Kingdom on Earth, His Church, which stands above all governments and all nations. Simultaneously, He healed all wounds and all diseases. He found both the strength and the time for all mankind and, finally, He opened up the Tsar-like Road of the Cross, which leads to His Kingdom in Heaven. He accomplished all this.

Of course, God could have done so directly, with a single act of His Omnipotent Desire. Yet He desired to do so by means of human nature and it was with human lips that He uttered the immortal words: *"... heaven and earth shall pass away, but My words shall not pass away"* (Matthew 24:35).

The human mind served as the tool for all this, and brought forth visions of the Divine, which were then made real. God knows not weariness, yet God-made-man waxed right weary in both soul and body. He hath earned his rest. Yet before taking His rest for all time, Jesus commended to His Father a great gift, His Holy Human Soul: *"Father! Into Thy Hands I commend my spirit"* (Luke 23:46).

Before proceeding further, I should like to instruct you to contemplate the beauty of the Soul Jesus Christ commended into the Hands of His Father. For thirty-three years, He lived only for the glory of the Father: *"Father, glorify Thy name"* (John 12:28). He burned with the desire to give unto the people an understanding of God and to aid them in loving Him. *"Now this is eternal life, that they may know thee, the only true God, and Jesus Christ, whom thou hast sent"* (John 17:3). His food was to do the will of His Father: *"My meat is to do the will of him that sent me, that I may perfect his work"* (John 4:34). His thirst was for the salvation and perfection of souls in unity with love: *"... that they may be one as we also are one, I in them and thou in me; that they may be made perfect in one"* (John 17:22–23). He loved and desired to suffer for our sake: *"And I have a baptism wherewith I am to be baptized, and how am I straitened until it be accomplished?"* (Luke 12:50). He strived to open the paths to life and true happiness before us. The beauty of all the angels, both Cherubim and Seraphim, shall not compare with the beauty of the Soul Christ commended into the Hands of His Father. *"Father, into Thy Hands I commend My Spirit."*

And now His Soul, sorrowful unto death, has entered into Great Repose. Yet think not that this is quietism or inaction. No. God is Pure, Simple, and Undivided Action. The Soul of Christ, which is the closest of all human souls to the Image and Likeness of God, proceeds to glorify God and to do good. He shall descend into the place of quiet, coolness, and light, where the souls that remain faithful to grace await the coming of their Savior, the conqueror of death and hell. His Body hath borne all things: the weight of the heat of the day and the torment of labor beyond endurance. He hath bent beneath the weight and shame of the Cross and hath been beaten and tormented by the hands of those for whom He suffered. This Body shall be laid in a new tomb hewn from the rock, and there He shall rest at Great Repose until the bright dawn of the Third Day. In His Countenance, that of God fallen asleep, is such peace and calm: *"And there came a great calm"* (Matthew 8:26). *"'Father, into Thy hands I commend my spirit.' And saying this, He gave up the ghost."* (Luke 23:46)

There came a great calm—such is the condition in the life of our souls that corresponds to Our Lord's Last Word in His Testament from the Cross. And how logically this proceeds. When He appeared on the earth the angels sang, *"Peace to men of goodwill."*[27] As the hour of His voluntary suffering drew nigh, He wished to leave for His people His most precious gift. He said to His Disciples, *"Peace I leave with you, my peace I give to you"* (John 14:27).

Peace with Christ, peace with God, peace with our fellow creatures, and thus peace within ourselves are greatly needed for our souls. Yet there are two kinds of peace. One is the peace of the Christian soul that conscientiously and honestly fulfills her duties in relation to God and her neighbor. She shall not permit herself to sin willfully and feels a peace of conscience through doing her duty before God and man. This also is peace with Christ and is a priceless gift to men of goodwill. Yet it is not of this peace that I wish to speak to you, for there is another form of peace. The struggle upon Golgotha and all moments in the life of our souls about which I have spoken precede it. This is more than the peace of a righteous conscience, this, rather, is peace of the spirit, of the highest regions of the soul, and the Mystical Peace of Christ.

27   (Cf. Luke 2:14)—The Editor.

The words of victory, "It is consumed," have pierced like a two-edged sword to the peak of the soul, and she has begun to act with a liberated and empowered will. There has come a Great Calm as a result of this liberation of her will. Her emotions and passions have calmed and obediently bowed before their new master, the will.

Joyful and free, the soul has, like Mary Magdalene, taken her place at the feet of Jesus and listens to His commands. *"Father, into Thy hands I commend My spirit."* It makes no difference to her will what He shall command. She is free from desire, from the passions, and from the emotions. *"Have confidence. I have overcome the world"* (John 16:33). The soul has overcome the world together with Christ. She has overcome the flesh, the Devil, and her own self.

Now, she shall rest, free and serene, at the feet of Christ. She has need of nothing. *"Father, into Thy Hands I commend my spirit. I surrender all things into Thy hands. The time hath come for Thee to act in me, and to do with me what Thou wilt."* The soul has earned her rest together with Christ. The struggles have passed and there has come a Great Calm upon her.

The night is come, a time when all is still, as though awaiting something. The soul resembles the smooth and motionless surface of a lake and she silently awaits. At the dawn of the Third Day, after the Great Calm, the Sun of Love and Truth shall rise, bathing the whole lake in His rays. A new life of love and unity shall commence. Meanwhile, the lake has fallen silent and waits. Yet she knows that the Sun shall rise. *"Father, into your hands I commend my spirit."*

Do not think that this Great Calm and Silence are a passive dissolution into God. To our nature, such a quietism would be false and deceptive. This is not dissolution of the soul. Rather it is like to a centering, wherein all the qualities of the soul converge unto her center, the will. She is thus united in pure acts of faith, hope, and love together with God—her unchanging, simple, single point of support. It is love that comes and reigns first and makes the soul draw nigh to her Creator, Who is now her closest likeness and Who is Pure Action. The entirety of the soul, without division or lapses, pours herself out in a simple and singular act of self-giving: *"Father, into Thy Hands I commend My Spirit."* There has come a Great Calm and a Great Silence, the silence of the night before the coming of the cloudless and everlasting day. Nothing and no one may take this peace away from her.

"Who shall separate us from the love of Christ? Shall tribulation? Or distress? Or famine? Or nakedness or danger? Or the sword? ... But in all things we overcome, because of Him that hath loved us. For I am sure[28] *that neither death, nor life, nor angels, nor principalities, nor powers, nor things present, nor things to come, nor might, nor height, nor depth, nor any other creature, shall be able to separate us from the love of God which is in Christ Jesus Our Lord"* (Romans 8:35, 37–39).

And the activity and the life of Great Calm is entirely within the soul and at her most exalted level: *"The Kingdom of God is within you"* (Luke 17:21). She depends on nothing external. Circumstances and events of her exterior life may evoke tears, yet they like to tears of

28　Here is that state of calm and repose. —The Author.

compassion. They are the tears that Christ wept over a Jerusalem that was perishing for refusing God and persisting in evil. Such things shall not disrupt the calm within the soul, for in all these events and contradictions which affect her, she sees the wisdom and bounty of Divine Providence. Why would she worry, be agitated, doubtful, or not at peace? *"Father, into Thy Hands I commend My Spirit."* The soul is, in her entirety, in the hands of God.

The Lord has received her into His Beneficent and Strong Hands and she reposes upon His Breast, in peace, calm, and stillness. She needs nothing and fears nothing, for no one and nothing may detach her from Him. In theory, while the soul could still fall and leave Him, this practically never happens. He holds her firmly to Himself. He is God; strong and powerful, all-loving, and loyal. Everything has been given over into His Hands: *"Father, into Thy Hands I commend my spirit."*

The soul is at the dawn, at the threshold of unity and the fullness of life, and she awaits her time in peace and calm …

He shall come with the dawn of the Third Day, shining in glory, to lead the soul, joyful and free, into His Bridal Chamber. Yet He has left her to rest for a time. She has suffered together with her Crucified God. She has struggled and, in spite of all things; the pressures of the world, the flesh and the Devil, she has remained faithful. She has hoped. She has loved.

And now is her victory, having conquered the world. Now, together with her Lord, she has merited her rest.

The night is come. Around the cross *"a Great Calm"* has descended. It is the Sabbath Day, when the Lord rested from all His Works. Jesus gazes peacefully and clearly at the heavens and quietly says, as He did when a child: *"'Father, into Thy Hands I commend My Spirit.' And having said this, He bowed His Head and gave up the Ghost."*

Epilogue.

Try to receive your Easter Communion tomorrow under the Banner of the Cross, in Great Calm and with Peace of Soul: *"And there reigned a great stillness."* Will yourself to put aside all personal thoughts and cares. Immerse yourselves in the contemplation of peace and stillness, the peace of the Most Holy Soul and Most Pure Body of our dying God. Truly, what peace is therein, what calm, and what stillness! *"And there reigned a great stillness."* And precisely within this peace, when all our passions and undertakings are silenced, await the coming of Our Lord and God, with the action of your will now set free, even if only for a time. Prior to His coming strive to awaken within yourselves three dispositions: 1) Renunciation of the self and of the outside world. There is naught except God. *"He must increase: but I must decrease"* (John 3:30). 2) A pure desire to glorify Christ. *"Father ... glorify Thy Son"* (John 17:1). *"Hallowed be Thy Name"* (Matthew 6:9). And finally 3) Great gratitude for all God has given you, to all souls. Recall, before all else, that *"God so loved the world, that He gave His Only Begotten Son"* (John 3:16) and also that He is beauteous, omnipotent, and good.

And when you receive Him, place your soul firmly and decisively into the strong and loving hands of your Lord and God and with the intercession of the Most Pure Virgin Mary: *"Father, into Thy Hands I commend My Spirit"* (Luke 23:46).

Prayer for the Beatification of The Servant of God Mother Catherine Abrikosova, T.O.S.D.

O Lord God Almighty, Thy Son suffered on the Cross and died for the salvation of our souls. Imitating Him, Thy servant Mother Catherine loved Thee with her whole heart, served Thee faithfully in the face of persecution, and devoted her life unto Thine All Holy Church. Make her famous in the assembly of Thy Blessed, so that the example of her faithfulness and love shall shine before the world entire. I pray unto Thee through her intercession. Hear my request....
Through Christ Our Lord.
Amen.

Through the prayers of our Holy Fathers Lord Jesus Christ Our God have mercy on us!

For private prayer, outside of Holy Mass.

+Archbishop Tadeusz Kondrusiewicz, May 4, 2004.

The Postulator, Fr. Alexei Janushchev-Rumyantsev, wishes to be informed of any favors received.